THE MUSEUM OF THE CITY OF NEW YORK

Portraits of America

The Statue of Liberty

THE MUSEUM OF THE CITY OF NEW YORK

Portraits of America

The Statue of Liberty

Cara A. Sutherland

BARNES
&NOBLE
BOOKS
NEW YORK

A BARNES & NOBLE BOOK

© 2003 Barnes & Noble Publishing, Inc.

Library of Congress Cataloging-in-Publication Data

Sutherland, Cara.
    The Statue of Liberty / Cara A. Sutherland.
        p. cm. — (Portraits of America)
    Includes bibliographical references and index.
    ISBN 0-7607-3890-4
    1. Statue of Liberty (New York, N.Y.)—History—Pictorial works. 2. Statue of Liberty (New York, N.Y.)—History. I. Title. II. Series.
    F128.64.L6 S88 2003
    974.7'1—dc21

                                                                    2002038253

Editor: Hallie Einhorn
Art Director: Kevin Ullrich
Designers: Christine Heun and Michele Trombley
Photography Editor: Janice Ackerman
Digital Imaging: Daniel J. Rutkowski
Production Manager: Richela Fabian Morgan

Color separations by Bright Arts Graphics (S) Pte Ltd.
Printed and bound in China by C&C Offset Printing Co. Ltd.

10 9 8 7 6 5 4 3 2 1

About the Museum of the City of New York

The Museum of the City of New York is one of New York City's great cultural treasures—the first U.S. museum dedicated to the study of a single city. Founded in 1923, it presents the nearly four hundred–year evolution of one of history's most important metropolises through exhibitions, educational programs, and publications, and by collecting and preserving the artifacts that tell New York's remarkable stories.

The Museum's collection of 1.5 million objects reflects the diverse and dramatic history of New York City. In addition to prints and photographs, the Museum collects and preserves paintings and sculptures, costumes, theater memorabilia, decorative arts and furniture, police and fire fighting materials, toys made or used in New York, material related to the history of the port, and thousands of varied objects and documents that illuminate the lives of New Yorkers, past and present. Among the gems of the collections are gowns worn at George Washington's inaugural ball, New York's last surviving omnibus and one of its last Checker Cabs, archives of the work of renowned photographers Jacob A. Riis and Berenice Abbott, the world's largest collection of Currier & Ives prints, and pieces of the Times Square news "zipper."

Through its Department of Learning, the Museum offers programs to thousands of teachers and students from all five boroughs every year, including guided tours, teacher training, and its annual New York City History Day contest— the nation's largest urban history fair. Other activities for audiences of all ages include hands-on workshops, performances, book readings, scholarly conferences and lectures, films, and walking tours.

The Museum's rich collections and archives are available to the public for research. To learn how to explore the collections or how to order reproductions of images, visit the Museum's website at www.mcny.org. The website also features exhibition previews, up-to-date program information, an on-line Museum shop, virtual exhibitions, student aids, and information on how you can support the Museum's work.

MUSEUM OF THE
CITY OF NEW YORK
1220 Fifth Avenue
New York, NY 10029
(212) 534-1672
www.mcny.org

Contents

INTRODUCTION
An Inspiring Conversation 8

CHAPTER ONE
The Artist's Concept 16

CHAPTER TWO
A Formidable Task 24

CHAPTER THREE
An Engineering Marvel 36

CHAPTER FOUR
The People's Statue 48

CHAPTER FIVE
Liberty Arrives 60

CHAPTER SIX
A Welcoming Sight 76

CHAPTER SEVEN
Standing Watch 82

CHAPTER EIGHT
Destination Liberty 102

SOURCES 124

INDEX 127

Above: In 1905, Henry Greenwood Peabody (1855–1951) captured this image of the Statue of Liberty from New York Harbor. His view is similar to the one that immigrants had as they approached Ellis Island.

An Inspiring Conversation

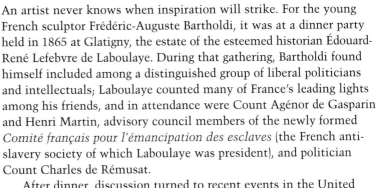

An artist never knows when inspiration will strike. For the young French sculptor Frédéric-Auguste Bartholdi, it was at a dinner party held in 1865 at Glatigny, the estate of the esteemed historian Édouard-René Lefebvre de Laboulaye. During that gathering, Bartholdi found himself included among a distinguished group of liberal politicians and intellectuals; Laboulaye counted many of France's leading lights among his friends, and in attendance were Count Agénor de Gasparin and Henri Martin, advisory council members of the newly formed *Comité français pour l'émancipation des esclaves* (the French anti-slavery society of which Laboulaye was president), and politician Count Charles de Rémusat.

After dinner, discussion turned to recent events in the United States: the Civil War, the abolition of slavery, and the assassination of President Abraham Lincoln. How could this young country maintain democracy in the face of adversity while France, founded on many of the same principles during its own revolutionary moment, had stumbled off the path? The conversation then shifted to the two republics' amicable relationship, which had been established during the American Revolution when the French gave financial and military support to the colonies struggling for independence. Laboulaye was a great admirer of the United States and was considered an expert on the nation and its constitution (he had published his three-volume *Histoire des États-Unis* [*History of the United States*] in 1855–1856). He argued that the friendship between the two countries should be celebrated through some kind of symbolic artwork—a gift from the people of France to the people of America. By the end of the evening, it would become Bartholdi's destiny to create this gift—a masterpiece honoring the mutual esteem held by the two cultures and the ideal of democracy.

It would be some time before a concrete plan took form. The project was tabled for several years, during which Bartholdi proved his skills as an artist. In 1866, he completed a bust of Laboulaye, which met with the scholar's approval. The following year, he was introduced to the khedive Isma'il Pasha during a visit to Paris by the Egyptian ruler. Bartholdi proposed an idea for the entrance to the Suez Canal: a massive lighthouse called *L'Égypte apportant la lumière à l'Asie* (Egypt Carrying the Light to Asia). In 1869, Bartholdi traveled to Egypt for the opening of the canal. He presented his drawings and a terra-cotta model to the khedive but was disappointed to learn that his proposal for the colossal statue was not to be implemented. The exercise was not in vain, however, for this design would

Above, left: Frédéric-Auguste Bartholdi (1834–1904) was a relatively unknown sculptor when he was tapped to design the Statue of Liberty, the masterpiece that would define his career. He produced a variety of works during his lifetime—fountains, bas-reliefs, statues, engravings—but would be remembered in history as Liberty's creator.

influence his later work. Bartholdi returned to France, where he enlisted in the military to fight in the Franco-Prussian War. In 1871, after he finished serving in the army, he found himself at another of Laboulaye's gatherings. During this get-together, Laboulaye reiterated his monumental idea to celebrate liberty, and he offered the artist the commission of a lifetime. Although the initial concept was Laboulaye's, Bartholdi convinced him to expand on the idea and create a colossus—a statue majestic enough to capture the world's attention.

Bartholdi set sail for the United States aboard the *Pereire* on June 8, 1871. His instructions from Laboulaye were to study the nation and its people; he was also directed to speak about Laboulaye's proposal for a monument of friendship in order to generate interest that would bolster the fund-raising efforts. The result of Bartholdi's journey would be the inspiration and determination to create his masterpiece, *Liberté éclairant le monde* (Liberty Enlightening the World), better known as the Statue of Liberty.

Opposite, right: Édouard-René Lefebvre de Laboulaye (1811–1883) conceived of the Statue of Liberty project as a means to commemorate the long-standing friendship between France and the United States.

Right: In the late 1860s, Bartholdi designed *L'Égypte apportant la lumière à l'Asie* (Egypt Carrying the Light to Asia), a lighthouse to be built at the entrance of the Suez Canal. The project never moved beyond the model stage but did serve as the artist's precedent for the idea of the colossal statue that would ultimately grace New York Harbor.

Right: Emphasizing its status as a symbol of freedom, the Statue of Liberty holds a tablet of law bearing, in Roman numerals, the date July 4, 1776—the day on which the Second Continental Congress adopted the Declaration of Independence. The tablet is two feet (0.6m) thick and nearly fourteen feet (4.3m) wide.

Left: In 1884, a group of Americans living in Paris ordered a thirty-six-foot (11m)-high bronze copy of the Statue of Liberty to give to their adopted city. The replica, produced by the foundry Thiébaut Frères, was based on one of Bartholdi's approved study models. The dedication ceremony took place on July 4, 1889, on the Pont de Grenelle, shortly before this photograph was taken, circa 1890, and about three years after the inauguration of the Statue of Liberty in New York Harbor. The replica remained in its original location until 1968, when the bridge was remodeled and the gift was relocated to its current Parisian address on the Île des Cygnes in the Seine.

Above: A German naval training ship sails by the Statue of Liberty in 1962.

Above: Many people feel that the Statue of Liberty is at the peak of its beauty in the darkness, when it stands illuminated in the midst of the harbor, as seen in this 1957 photograph.

Above: Bartholdi's studio was located in his house in Paris at 40, rue Vavin. Here he created the majority of his works, including models for the Statue of Liberty—one of which is seen at the center of this 1890s photograph. Bartholdi stands in the doorway.

CHAPTER ONE

The Artist's Concept

"Everything is big here, even the green peas!" So wrote Bartholdi about the wonders of the United States in a letter to Laboulaye on July 15, 1871. Bartholdi, who had arrived in New York Harbor on June 21, 1871, was on a mission for his mentor to determine a location and design for the commissioned statue.

Bartholdi's tour was reminiscent of one taken years earlier by his countryman Alexis de Tocqueville. Laboulaye provided Bartholdi with letters of introduction to a number of prominent Americans, and, during the course of his venture, Bartholdi enlisted support for the project from many of them. After visiting New York City, he traveled to Long Branch, New Jersey, where he met with President Ulysses S. Grant. Bartholdi then headed to New England to visit with the poet Henry Wadsworth Longfellow, who encouraged him to present the idea at the centennial celebration in 1876. On Independence Day, Bartholdi was in the nation's capital with Senator Charles Sumner of Massachusetts. While in Washington, D.C., he befriended another artist, painter John La Farge. Bartholdi returned to New York, then it was on to Philadelphia and Chicago, which he considered "the most American city." He continued to travel west, crossing the Rocky Mountains in late summer and visiting Salt Lake City, where he was introduced to Brigham Young, head of the Mormon church. Bartholdi's western tour continued with stops in Sacramento and San Francisco. By this point, he had traveled from coast to coast in search of inspiration and support. The return trip took him through Denver, St. Louis, Cincinnati, and Pittsburgh. After one last stop in Philadelphia to brainstorm about ideas for displaying the project at the centennial celebration to be held in that city, he returned to New York and set sail for France. Bartholdi had spent nearly four months in the United States, and it was time to report back to Laboulaye and begin the implementation of his ideas.

From the beginning, Bartholdi and Laboulaye pondered how best to represent the concept of liberty in human form. They found their inspiration in images used in the seal of France's Second Republic and on American coins of the early nineteenth century, both of which reflected the ideal of Libertas, the goddess of ancient Rome who personified personal freedom. Associated with Jupiter, Libertas was deified by the Romans in the fourth century B.C.E. and worshiped by a cross section of society, especially freed slaves. In the eighteenth century C.E., republican philosophers and artists inspired by classical ideals turned to Libertas as an allegorical symbol. By the time of Bartholdi's commission, Libertas was recognized in both France and

America as an emblem of freedom and was therefore acceptable to Laboulaye as a prototype for the statue.

Having an agreed-upon concept, Bartholdi could begin the modeling process. In recent years, there has been much speculation that the statue was intended to be symbolic of an African slave—thereby representing abolitionist sentiments—because of the broken shackle and chain lying at her feet. But in keeping with Laboulaye and Bartholdi's original source of inspiration for creating the statue, it is more likely that those items represent America's break from European control and its ability to maintain political independence in the years following the Revolution. Although dedication speeches in 1886 would praise the Union's victory in the Civil War and the abolition of slavery, the statue itself suggests a more general expression of political independence, in keeping with the intellectual climate of the time. For Bartholdi, inspiration for the statue's facial features came from a source much closer to home—his mother, Charlotte, whose visage is strikingly similar to that of the finished statue.

As Bartholdi worked on the design for the statue, he submitted various models for Laboulaye's approval. It took several years, but in 1875 Bartholdi achieved a design that would enable him to take the next step. He delivered this terra-cotta study model to Honoré Monduit of the Monduit and Béchet foundry for fabrication review. Just over four feet (1.2m) tall, the maquette would be used to develop the proportions of the final statue—which would tower over New York Harbor at a height of more than 150 feet (45.7m).

Right: Although unsigned, this nineteenth-century map of New York Harbor is thought to be the work of Bartholdi. Someone familiar with the French language created the map, as the compass symbol for west is "O," which stands for *ouest*—the French word for that direction. The large dot located above the word *Bay* marks the location of Bedloe's Island, Bartholdi's preferred placement for the Statue of Liberty. And the curving dotted line highlights the path of incoming ships entering the harbor and passing by Bedloe's Island— which would indeed become the site of the statue—on their way into port.

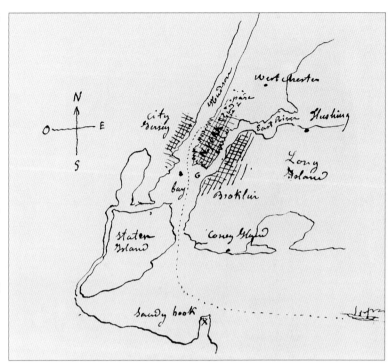

Opposite, bottom: Currier & Ives produced the print *Port of New York: Bird's Eye View from the Battery Looking South* based on artwork by Charles R. Parsons and Lyman Atwater. In this circa 1872 view, the Hudson River stretches toward the sea, the boroughs of Brooklyn and Staten Island visible from the Manhattan shore. This is the harbor as Bartholdi would have seen it during his first visit. The small bit of land right of center is Bedloe's Island.

Left: This rough terra-cotta model (circa 1870) is believed to represent Bartholdi's initial thoughts on the Statue of Liberty. The figure bears an incomplete torch in its right hand and is attired in classical drapery with chains at its feet. In its left hand is an undefined fragment.

Right: In this later terra-cotta model of the statue (circa 1870–1871), Bartholdi has incorporated the idea of a radiant crown. However, he is still uncertain about what to do with the left hand and has it holding a broken chain.

Left: By 1875, Bartholdi is nearing completion of his vision and has figured out what to do with Liberty's left hand: in it, the artist has put a tablet of law inscribed with the date of America's independence.

Above: Following a successful display at the Philadelphia Centennial Exhibition, Liberty's torch was brought to New York City in early 1877 and installed in Madison Square Park, named in honor of James Madison, fourth president of the United States (1809–1817).

CHAPTER TWO

A Formidable Task

How to go from just over 4 feet (1.2m) to more than 150 feet (45.7m)? That was the challenge Bartholdi posed to the foundry in charge of casting his grand design. Certainly history had proven that colossal statues could be built. Consider what the Egyptians had done with stone. And of course there was the legendary Colossus of Rhodes, one of the Seven Wonders of the World. Reportedly made of cast bronze and reaching over 105 feet (32m) high, this figure also stood at the entrance to a harbor. The marvel was constructed in the third century B.C.E. as a tribute to Helios, Greek god of the sun, but presided for only a few generations before being toppled by an earthquake. Although known only from written descriptions, this giant monument carried a torch of freedom and wore a crown of rays—elements that Bartholdi would incorporate into his modern wonder of the world.

While the craftsmen at the Monduit and Béchet foundry pondered their new assignment, Bartholdi and his patron had a more pressing problem—how to pay for the project. Drawing on his professional experience and social connections, Laboulaye established in 1875 the Franco-American Union, a fund-raising organization dedicated to seeing the statue through from design to completion. As with the statue itself, the union was a joint effort of the two countries and was directed by private citizens—it was not run by either government. The plan was for the French to pay for the statue, while the Americans would build the pedestal and cover the installation expenses. Laboulaye served as president of the Franco-American Union, as well as chairman of the French national committee, based in Paris.

On September 28, 1875, the Franco-American Union's fund-raising appeal appeared in French newspapers. After presenting the idea of the grand statue, the piece went on to say: "We will in this way declare by an imperishable memorial the friendship that the blood spilled by our fathers sealed of old between the two nations." The notice was also distributed widely in America, and on October 15, 1875, it appeared in the *New York Tribune* along with a letter from Laboulaye stating that the gift expressed France's wish to recognize "that noble liberty which represents the glory of the United States, and which enlightens the modern people by its example."

On November 6, 1875, Bartholdi unveiled his final design at a fund-raising banquet at the Hôtel du Louvre in Paris. The evening was a success, and a sum of 40,000 francs was contributed—10 percent of the estimated 400,000 francs needed to build the statue. By the end of the year, more than 200,000 francs had been raised, and

25

work on the statue could commence. Bartholdi, accompanied by architect Eugène-Emmanuel Viollet-le-Duc, returned to Monduit and Béchet to discuss the details and finalize a construction plan. They also decided that they wanted to have the upper portion of Liberty's right arm, bearing the torch, completed in time to be displayed at the opening of the Philadelphia Centennial Exhibition—less than six months away—to help spark interest in the project in America and bolster the fund-raising efforts there.

Viollet-le-Duc, who was chosen to design the statue's internal structure, was one of Bartholdi's former instructors. He was known for his restoration work in France, including that of Nôtre Dame Cathedral in Paris. Working with his one-time pupil, he conceived the idea of using a hollow wooden framework, against the exterior of which copper sheets would be hammered into shape—a technique known as repoussé. These shaped copper pieces would then be removed and attached to each other against a permanent framework of iron armature bars providing support for the finished statue. Additional internal support would be provided by a series of sand-filled coffers rising from the base to hip level, lending stability to the finished statue. With the basic structural decisions made, work began in earnest. An estimated twenty craftsmen, laboring ten hours a day, seven days a week, struggled to complete the right arm and torch by the April 1876 deadline. But they did not finish their task until June. And it was July before the thirty-seven-foot (11.3m) segment was shipped to America.

While work was progressing on the statue, Bartholdi returned to the United States, this time in an official capacity as a French delegate to the Philadelphia Centennial Exhibition. Bartholdi set sail aboard the *Amérique* on May 6, 1876. Upon his arrival in the States, he spent several weeks in Philadelphia reviewing installation plans. But the real purpose of his visit was to jump-start the American fund-raising efforts for the statue's pedestal. In the course of this endeavor, he made several trips to New York City. On Independence Day, he visited Bedloe's Island—the proposed site for the statue—with potential donors; by early August, he was back in Philadelphia waiting for the arm and torch to arrive. The crates were there by the middle of that month, and the pieces were quickly assembled for viewing. Bartholdi then returned to New York to participate in the September 6, 1876, unveiling of another monument he had created to celebrate the friendly relations between the United States and France—a statue of the Marquis de Lafayette, the French aristocrat who fought on the side of the colonists in the American Revolution.

During this early September visit, Bartholdi convinced the individuals who had been involved with raising funds for the installation of the Lafayette statue to take on the Liberty project as the New York branch of the Franco-American Union. Upon learning of this development, citizens of Philadelphia established their own local fund-raising committee in hopes that New York efforts would fail

AS SOON AS I HEARD OF
AMERICAN INDEPENDENCE
MY HEART
WAS ENLISTED
1776.

and the Centennial City would end up with the entire statue to call its own. But the artist preferred New York, and he focused his energies there. His persistence was rewarded on January 2, 1877, when the members of the influential Union League of New York agreed to coordinate the efforts of the various local committees and established the American Committee of the Franco-American Union. With the fund-raising structure in place, it was time for Bartholdi to return to France. But this time, he was not traveling alone. In between all of his official tasks, he had found time to court and marry Jeanne-Emilie Baheux du Puysieux, a young Frenchwoman he had met on his first American visit in 1871.

As Frédéric-Auguste and Jeanne-Emilie settled into married life, American efforts to secure public commitment to the statue made progress. Upon the close of the Centennial Exhibition, the French Committee of the Franco-American Union provided funds to ship the arm and torch from Philadelphia to New York. There, in early 1877, the city's Department of Public Works installed it in Madison Square Park, where the American Committee could showcase it for the pedestal campaign. On February 22 of that year, the United States House of Representatives voted to accept Liberty Enlightening the World as a gift from the French people. The Senate echoed this approval in a vote taken within a week, and days later, President Ulysses S. Grant signed the official paperwork. With federal approval, the project was now guaranteed a site and funds for its maintenance. Armed with this good news and financial commitment from the statue's sponsors, Bartholdi established the next goal: to complete Liberty's head in time for the Paris Universal Exposition of 1878. He returned to the Monduit and Béchet foundry to begin work on the new phase.

While Liberty's head was being constructed, Bartholdi and Laboulaye continued the French fund-raising campaign. Following the initial success in late 1875, when 50 percent of the estimated costs had been secured, financial contributions slowed considerably and subsequent fund-raising events failed to produce the sum needed to complete the statue. It was time for some creative thinking. Bartholdi had a brainstorm for the summer season of 1877. He created a diorama of the statue standing in New York Harbor for installation at the Palais de l'Industrie. For a small fee, visitors could view Bartholdi's vision of the statue, as it would stand on Bedloe's Island. The installation was such a success that it was moved to a more prominent Paris location, the Tuileries Garden, where it remained on display until 1879. But the key event would be the unveiling of Liberty's head at the Paris Universal Exposition in 1878. Bartholdi and Laboulaye understood the value of public drama in fund-raising. Upon the head's completion at the foundry, it was transported in a celebratory parade through the streets of Paris to its destination on the Champs de Mars. The official unveiling occurred on July 16, 1878, and during the course of the exposition, thousands of people took their turn climbing the thirty-six steps to the crown.

Opposite: Bartholdi began work on *Lafayette Arriving in America* shortly after returning from his first trip to the United States in 1871. Commissioned by the French government, the statue was designed to honor America's support of France during the Franco-Prussian War. It was unveiled on September 6, 1876, in New York City's Union Square, where it remains today.

As the French fund-raising efforts gained momentum, change was in the air. Metalworkers Emile Gaget and J.B. Gauthier, who had joined the firm of Monduit and Béchet as partners in January 1874, bought out Honoré Monduit in 1878 and renamed the foundry Gaget, Gauthier et Companie. The following year, a serious and unexpected setback occurred. Architect Viollet-le-Duc became ill in the summer of 1879 and died on September 17. Bartholdi suddenly needed to hire a replacement. He turned to well-known engineer Alexandre-Gustave Eiffel.

Below: This collector's edition is one of two hundred Modèle du Comité statuettes issued by the Franco-American Union to raise money for the Statue of Liberty. The terra-cotta figure was based on Bartholdi's *modèle d'étude* (study model) used in the final planning stages of the statue.

Above: On November 21, 1877, former U.S. president Ulysses S. Grant visited Monduit and Béchet to see how the statue was progressing. (Grant is the man in the top hat standing closer to center.) The stop in Paris was part of a two-year world tour that he embarked on in May 1877, following his second term as president. Grant had been a crucial supporter of the project, signing the government's acceptance of the French gift on March 3, 1877—his last day in office.

Right: Liberty's head was the second portion of the statue to be completed. As with the torch, the deadline was driven by a desire for public display to assist with the fund-raising efforts. This illustration from the French newspaper *Journal Universel* shows craftsmen hard at work to ready the head for the Paris Universal Exposition of 1878.

Opposite: On July 16, 1878, Liberty's head was unveiled at the Paris Universal Exposition. Visitors to the attraction were enthralled by their close-up view of the statue in progress. Like their American counterparts experiencing the arm and torch at the Philadelphia Centennial Exhibition and later in Madison Square Park in New York City, tourists happily paid a small fee to climb inside.

Above: Craftsmen used the repoussé technique to create the "skin" for Liberty. An estimated 200,000 pounds (90,800kg) of copper was needed to complete the statue. The majority of it—128,000 pounds (58,100kg)—was donated by Pierre-Eugène Secrétan, an industrialist who made his fortune in copper production during the 1870s. He would lose his wealth in the copper crash of 1889, when the British flooded the international market with copper and the metal's price collapsed.

CHAPTER THREE

An Engineering Marvel

Alexandre-Gustave Eiffel was known for his railway bridges and viaducts when he signed on as Bartholdi's structural engineer. Although he kept Viollet-le-Duc's original plans for a copper repoussé exterior, he had other ideas for the statue's internal framework. Borrowing tried-and-true ideas from his railroad projects, Eiffel devised a new support system, which he presented to Bartholdi in 1880. Instead of sand-filled coffers, Eiffel's proposal consisted of a ninety-two-foot (28m)-high pylon structure composed of four iron weight-bearing posts with a single forty-foot (12.2m) iron beam attached to support the raised arm and torch. In the center would be a double-spiral staircase. Connected to the pylon creation would be a second-ary structure of trusswork, to which the repoussé elements would be fastened with a system of iron bars and rivets. This armature system would offer a certain amount of flexibility, allowing the copper sheets to expand and contract with seasonal temperature shifts. The idea was approved, and Eiffel supervised its construction in the foundry yard, completing the project in 1881. Four years later, Eiffel was contracted to create his own masterwork: the centerpiece for the Paris World's Fair of 1889. Nearly one thousand feet (305m) high, the Eiffel Tower held the record as the world's tallest "building" until 1930, when it surrendered its title to New York City's Chrysler Building.

While Eiffel focused on the statue's support structure, Bartholdi and his assistant, Marie Simon, worked on creating the body parts for assembly. Beginning with a terra-cotta prototype slightly larger than four feet (1.2m), they created wood-and-plaster models using a method called "pointing," which entails establishing detailed reference points in order to create a series of enlarged models (Liberty would need a total of four models, including the terra-cotta original, to reach her final size). By the time the final model had been produced, Bartholdi estimated that more than nine thousand measurements had been taken for each stage of enlargement. First the statue grew from just over 4 feet (1.2m) to about 9 feet (2.7m) tall; then it jumped to nearly 36 feet (11m). It ended its spurt at 111 feet (33.8m), to which the extended arm and torch would be added, completing the height at 151 feet (46m). Once the full-size model was finished, carpenters and wood-carvers followed its details to create a series of wooden forms against which the metalworkers would hammer out the copper repoussé skin of the statue. When finished, Liberty would boast more than 350 individual copper pieces, held together by thousands of rivets.

The actual statue was constructed in segments. As each portion was completed, it was then attached to the iron framework located

outside in the foundry yard. Month by month, the statue began to take shape. As it grew over the rooftops of the foundry, it became a tourist attraction, and 25 rue de Chazelles—the location of Gaget, Gauthier et Companie—became a famous address. An estimated 300,000 people visited the spot during the course of the statue's assembly.

In August 1882, as the statue neared completion, the arm and torch were deinstalled in New York and shipped back to Paris. By the end of 1883, all of the components were nearly finished. The statue debuted in final form in January 1884. On July 4 of that year the Statue of Liberty was presented to Levi Parsons Morton, American minister to France, in a formal ceremony held in the foundry yard. On behalf of the French people, Viscount Ferdinand Marie de Lesseps, the new president of the Franco-American Union, remarked: "We commit it to your care, Mr. Minister, that it may remain forever the pledge of the bonds which should unite France and the great American nation." Bartholdi then led the dignitaries up the double staircase inside the statue. The celebration continued throughout the day, ending with a banquet. But there was an empty seat at the table, for Laboulaye, whose vision had guided the project for nearly twenty years, had died on May 25, 1883.

In the coming months, the statue would be carefully documented, disassembled, and packed into shipping crates. It was now time for the journey to its new home.

Opposite: Alexandre-Gustave Eiffel (1832–1923) was a skilled railroad bridge engineer when Bartholdi hired him to work on the Statue of Liberty. His experience with the statue would serve him well in later years when he created his own masterpiece—the Eiffel Tower—for the Paris World's Fair of 1889.

Left: Workmen construct a final wood-and-plaster model of Liberty's left hand. The craftsman at center is covered with dust from the process. Below the arm are two men having a discussion; the one on the left is believed to be Bartholdi.

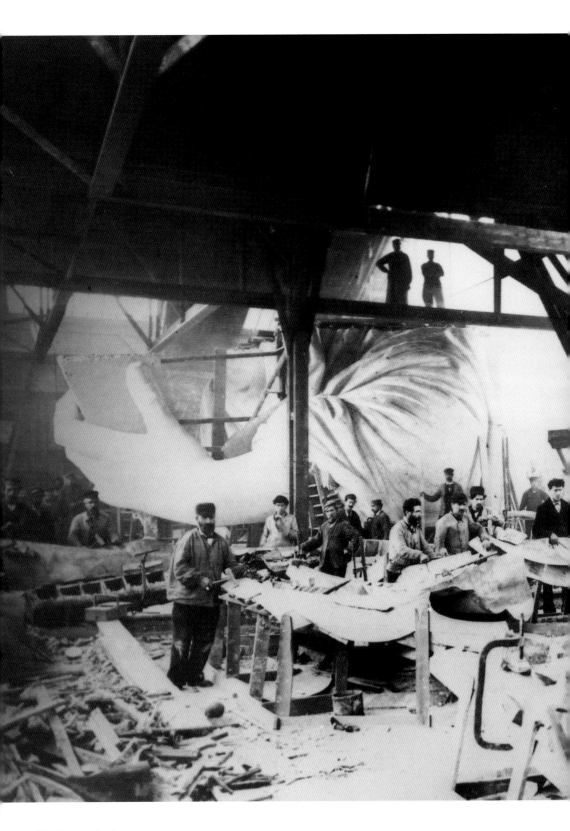

Left: Workmen stop to pose with their finished product—Liberty's left hand and arm. The model is now ready to be used for creating the repoussé molds. Note the smaller model of the left arm and hand, as well as one of Liberty's head, in the back right corner.

Opposite: Liberty's head was on display outside the foundry during an event held on October 24, 1881, to celebrate the installation of the first rivets attaching copper repoussé sheets to the statue's armature. On hand were representatives of the French and American governments. U.S. diplomat Levi Parsons Morton had the honor of driving the first rivet into Liberty's armature.

Above: Little by little, the statue grew from the ground up. The metal structure extending upward would eventually provide support for Liberty's right arm and torch. On December 19, 1882, Bartholdi wrote to William M. Evarts, chair of the American Committee of the Franco-American Union, "The statue commences to reach above the houses, and next spring will see it overlook the entire city."

Right: Liberty was almost complete when this photograph was taken in 1883. Many would come to visit the statue during the course of construction and in the months following its completion. On November 29, 1884, Bartholdi was honored by a visit from the poet and novelist Victor Hugo, to whom he gave a piece of copper repoussé engraved with the date of the writer's visit. Nearly six months later, on May 13, 1885, Hugo wrote to Bartholdi: "To the sculptor, form is everything and nothing—nothing without the spirit, everything with the idea."

Opposite: This close-up view shows the workmen's entrance in the sole of Liberty's upraised right foot.

FRANK LESLIE'S ILLUSTRATED NEWSPAPER

Entered according to Act of Congress, in the year 1885, by Mrs. Frank Leslie, in the Office of the Librarian of Congress at Washington.—Entered at the Post Office, New York, N.Y., as Second-class Matter

No. 1,551.—Vol. LX.]   NEW YORK—FOR THE WEEK ENDING JUNE 13, 1885.   [Price, 10 Cents.

1. OFFICIAL PRESENTATION OF THE STATUE OF "LIBERTY ENLIGHTENING THE WORLD," PARIS, JULY 4TH, 1884.   2. M. FRÉDÉRIC-AUGUSTE BARTHOLDI.
3. SECTIONAL VIEW OF STATUE, SHOWING IRON CORE AND BRACES.—SEE PAGE 271.
FRANCE-AMERICA.—THE GIFT OF THE FRENCH REPUBLIC TO THE UNITED STATES.

Opposite: On July 4, 1884, the Franco-American Union presented the completed Statue of Liberty to the American people. The ceremony was held in the foundry yard of Gaget, Gauthier et Companie with numerous politicians and dignitaries in attendance—some of whom signed the official transfer document, shown here.

Left: The illustration at left on this page from the June 13, 1885, edition of *Frank Leslie's Illustrated Newspaper* documents the presentation of the completed Statue of Liberty to the American people in Paris. Levi Parsons Morton, who had already enjoyed the honor of driving in the first rivet, accepted the gift on behalf of his country. Morton later went on to serve as vice president (1889–1893) under Benjamin Harrison and governor of New York (1895–1897).

Above: The pedestal foundation, made of poured concrete, was a massive project. An estimated 200 to 250 barrels of concrete were used each day to construct the 11,680-cubic-yard foundation. The concrete was transported to the site via a railway system built for the project.

CHAPTER FOUR

The People's Statue

Boston? Philadelphia? New York? While members of the French Committee of the Franco-American Union celebrated the end of their fund-raising activities and watched the statue's construction progress to completion, their American counterparts struggled to come up with funds to pay for the pedestal. Although Bartholdi's chosen location was New York Harbor, Liberty's home seemed, for a time, to be up for grabs. Boston made a play for the statue in 1882, which not surprisingly, upset New Yorkers. The *New York Times* published a vehement response to this perceived attack on the city's honor in an October 3, 1882, editorial: "We have more than a million people in this City who are resolved that that...statue shall be smashed into minute fragments before it shall be stuck up in Boston Harbor. If we are to lose the statue it shall go to some worthier and more modest place—Painted Post, for instance, or Glover, Vt."

What had gone wrong with the American effort? When Bartholdi ended his second visit in January 1877, the New York sponsors were certain of their future success. After all, the American Committee needed to raise only half as much as the French in order to pay for its part—the pedestal. But because the Americans perceived their share of the project as minimal, fund-raising did not begin in earnest until late 1881, when they realized that a considerable amount of money was still needed in order to move forward with the pedestal design and keep the statue's construction schedule on track.

On December 6, 1881, the American Committee contracted Richard Morris Hunt to design the pedestal. Hunt, a New York architect trained at Paris's École des Beaux-Arts, was known for his residential work on New York's Stuyvesant Apartments (1869–1870) and Roosevelt Building (1873–1874). He shared Bartholdi's views on the grandeur of the project, and his first proposal was for a massive base, nearly 115 feet (35m) tall and estimated to cost $250,000—twice what the Americans had budgeted for the entire pedestal project. Because of these financial constraints, Hunt went back to the drawing board to create a scaled-back design. While he continued on the redesign, excavation and site work were taking place at Fort Wood, the old military base on Bedloe's Island. The construction team broke ground in April 1883 and began work on the concrete foundation on October 9 of that year. The foundation was completed on May 17, 1884, and when those bills were totaled, the cost came in at $93,830.94—twice the amount originally budgeted for that portion of the pedestal project. Hunt's revised design called for an eighty-nine-foot (27m)-high pedestal of solid granite. But because of the ongoing

Right: The pedestal's corner-stone-laying ceremony took place on August 5, 1884, a rainy summer day. Grand Master William A. Brodie of the Grand Lodge of New York presided over the event, which began with the placing of the six-ton (5.4t) block into position. A number of the men involved with the Liberty project belonged to the Freemasons, a fraternal organization with roots in eighteenth-century Enlightenment thought. Both Bartholdi and Laboulaye were Freemasons, as was Richard Morris Hunt, the pedestal's architect.

budget problems, Hunt was asked to come up with a less expensive alternative, so he settled on poured concrete with granite block facing. That plan was accepted on August 7, 1884, two days after the corner-stone had been laid. For his efforts, Hunt was paid $1,000, which he returned as a contribution to the fund-raising campaign. Following his work on the Statue of Liberty, Hunt would go on to create estates for the Vanderbilt family—Biltmore (1888–1895) in Asheville, North Carolina, and the Breakers (1892–1895) in Newport, Rhode Island. He died in 1895, seven years before his public masterpiece, New York's Metropolitan Museum of Art (1894–1902), was completed.

Unfortunately, most members of the American Committee did not demonstrate the generosity shown by Hunt. Originally a small group of twenty-two people drawn from the ranks of high society, the committee boasted four hundred members by the 1882–83 social season. While they organized various fund-raising events, they were not so free with their own money. On October 8, 1883, newspaper publisher Joseph Pulitzer denounced this lack of commitment in his New York *World*: "We have more than a hundred millionaires in this city, any one of whom might have written a check for the whole sum….Towards a foreign ballet dancer…their hearts and pockets would have opened. But do they care for a Statue of Liberty, which only reminds them of the equality of all citizens of the Republic?"

Pulitzer had thrown down a gauntlet to New York society and America at large. He was a Hungarian immigrant and self-made newspaperman who used his publications to promote his favored causes. Throughout 1884, Pulitzer wrote about and crusaded for the Statue of Liberty. He celebrated when the pedestal cornerstone was laid in early August and despaired the following winter when construction was halted due to a lack of funds. By 1885, his frustration at the American Committee's slow progress seemed to reach its peak. Pulitzer learned that at a March 12 committee finance meeting it had been revealed that there was only $2,866.89 left in the bank. Four days later, in an editorial, he announced his own pedestal campaign. He argued that since the statue was being built with contributions from French laborers, members of America's working class should prove that they could be equal to the task by providing funds for Liberty's "footstool," as he referred to the pedestal. Pulitzer urged his readers to give what they could, no matter how small the amount. To further encourage participation, he promised to publish the name of every person who donated money to the cause, regardless of the size of the sum.

The people heard his call, and the money came pouring in—more than $2,000 in the first week alone. The donations frequently included notes, which Pulitzer published as further incentive to his readers. "This inclosed [sic] dollar comes from a party of poor artists," wrote one donor. Another gave "five cents as a poor office boy's mite toward the Pedestal Fund." Comments ranged from the serious to the humorous; one donor revealed, "Since leaving smoking cigarettes I have gained twenty-five pounds, so I cheerfully enclose a penny for each pound. Having increased my own stature, I donate this to the Statue of Liberty." Even children made contributions; one group sent one dollar, describing their donation as "the money we saved to go to the circus with." Some people could not send money but instead sent items for Pulitzer to sell to add to the pedestal coffers.

By the end of the second week of the campaign, Pulitzer revealed that 2,535 donors had contributed a total of $3,359.67, including the initial $1,000 put up by Pulitzer himself. On April 15, the total was up to $25,762.36, and on April 17, Pulitzer sent a first installment of $25,000 to the American Committee. By the end of May, a second check for $25,000 was on its way to the fund-raising group, and on August 11, less than five months after his editorial announcing the beginning of the newspaper's fund-raising efforts, Pulitzer declared in the *World* that $100,000 had been raised for Liberty's pedestal. The campaign was finished, and it had been a complete success; the people of America had responded in kind to the people of France. Thanks to the contributions of patriotic citizens, work on the pedestal resumed; it was finished by April 1886.

Left: Workmen pose next to the almost completed pedestal foundation on Bedloe's Island. Work on the foundation began on October 9, 1883, and continued until May 17, 1884. The laborers, most of whom were Italian immigrants, lived on the island through the winter.

Right: The American Committee of the Franco-American Union held numerous events to raise money for Liberty's pedestal. One of their most successful ventures was an afternoon of entertainment at the Casino Theatre in New York City on April 7, 1885.

Right: Joseph Pulitzer (1847–1911) made it his business to raise money for the statue's pedestal. Using his resources as publisher of the New York *World*, he launched his own fund-raising campaign on March 16, 1885.

Left: On August 11, 1885, the *World* proudly announced the end of the newspaper's fund-raising campaign. In less than five months, the paper raised in excess of $100,000, enough to finish the Statue of Liberty's pedestal. More than 120,000 individuals contributed to the cause, making it truly "the people's statue."

Below: Curiosity drove visitors to Bedloe's Island before Liberty had even arrived. The sightseers in this image are riding an excursion boat that was part of the American Committee's endeavor to raise money for the statue's pedestal. Photographer George B. Brainerd took this shot on June 25, 1885. Following the dedication and opening of the Statue of Liberty, the profits from the ferry service were used for the monument's upkeep.

Above: Seated on Liberty's pedestal foundation is photographer Wallace G. Levison, who accompanied fellow photographer George B. Brainerd on his June 25, 1885, trip to the island. Brainerd took the shot.

Left: Visitors to Bedloe's Island in June of 1885 saw an only partially completed pedestal, as work had been suspended due to a lack of funds. Nonetheless, the site offered a grand view of New York Harbor, as captured in this image by Wallace G. Levison.

Above: Thousands of people witnessed the festivities surrounding the statue's dedication on October 28, 1886. At the moment of unveiling, which accidentally occurred prematurely, Liberty was given a gun salute by many of the ships in the harbor.

CHAPTER FIVE

Liberty Arrives

While Americans fretted about pedestal politics, the French prepared the statue for its voyage to the New World. Liberty was disassembled in January 1885 and carefully packed into 214 numbered crates. A special train with seventy cars was used to transport the crates from Paris to the port of Rouen, where it took seventeen days to load them onto the *Isère*, the French naval ship commissioned for this special assignment. The *Isère* set sail on May 21, 1885, and nearly four weeks later, after a stormy and rocky crossing, Liberty entered New York Harbor, where she was greeted with much fanfare on June 17.

Liberty had arrived. The crates were off-loaded onto shuttle boats and brought to Bedloe's Island for storage. It would be another ten months before the pedestal was complete and the assembly could begin. On October 24, 1885, Bartholdi boarded the steamship *Amérique* and headed for New York himself. The purpose of this visit was to meet with the chief engineer for the statue's assembly, General Charles Pomeroy Stone, and review the plan. Once again, the American Committee fêted Bartholdi. This visit was relatively brief, and on November 25, he departed New York on the *Normandie* and returned to Paris. The project was now in American hands, and Bartholdi would not come back until the statue was ready for unveiling.

Stone had a formidable task facing him. The goodwill of two nations rested on his shoulders. A graduate of West Point, an army veteran, and an experienced civil engineer, Stone had overseen the building of the statue's pedestal. Following its completion in April 1886, he began work on joining the various parts of the statue's iron pylon and armature system. By August, it was time to begin attaching the copper repoussé panels to the skeleton. The first two rivets ceremonially driven through a copper sheet and into the framework were dubbed "Bartholdi" and "Pulitzer." Within a matter of months, it was time to attach Liberty's head. In early October 1886, the statue was virtually complete, and renowned landscape architect Frederick Law Olmsted—designer of New York's Central Park—supervised the site cleanup in preparation for the dedication ceremony on October 28.

As the Americans readied the statue for the ceremony, Bartholdi, his wife, and numerous French dignitaries traveled to Le Havre and boarded the steamship *Bretagne* on October 17. They arrived in New York on October 25 and were celebrated at several events. Two days later, Mayor William R. Grace presented Bartholdi with the "Freedom of the City" (a document that was the nineteenth-century equivalent of the keys to the city). But the real honor for the artist was to see his completed statue standing tall in the harbor. As reported

Above: The French ship *Isère* arrived in New York Harbor on June 17, 1885, loaded with 214 crates containing the individual components of the disassembled Statue of Liberty.

by the *New York Times* on October 28, 1886, Bartholdi stated: "My dream has been realized. I can only say that I am enchanted. This thing will live to eternity when we shall have passed away, and everything living with us has moldered away."

Festivity was in the air on the morning of October 28. It was a day when New Yorkers and the world would celebrate friendship and liberty. Although the sky was cloudy and there was the threat of rain, nothing could dampen the spirits of those involved with the project. It had taken more than twenty years, but Bartholdi and Laboulaye's vision, formulated at a dinner party in 1865, had become a reality.

The elaborate celebration boasted a series of events. An estimated one million people turned out to watch Grand Marshal Charles Pomeroy Stone, who had become intimately familiar with the statue as he supervised the final assembly of Lady Liberty on-site, lead a parade down 5th Avenue. At around 11:30 A.M., it reached Madison Square Park, between 23rd and 26th Streets, where the marchers—an estimated twenty thousand—were greeted from a receiving stand by President Grover Cleveland. Decorated floats, marching bands, army regiments, firemen, and politicians passed by that stand. The parade eventually turned onto Broadway and headed toward the waterfront, where more than three hundred vessels of all shapes and sizes waited in the harbor to participate in a parade of ships honoring the statue.

By 1:00 P.M., the second portion of the day was beginning. President Cleveland reviewed the ships from aboard the *Despatch* before landing on Bedloe's Island with a select group of two thousand guests. At 3:15 P.M., the dedication ceremony began. The Reverend Richard S. Storrs gave the opening prayer. Then Viscount Ferdinand de Lesseps, Laboulaye's successor as president of the Franco-American Union, addressed the crowd, followed by Senator William M. Evarts of New York, chairman of the American Committee. A bit of confusion ensued as a mistaken signal resulted in Bartholdi's pulling the cord and prematurely unveiling the statue. The harbor erupted with sound as the naval ships began their gun salutes, and the flotilla responded with a symphony of steam whistles; onlookers on land and aboard the ships cheered their approval. Once the crowd settled down, President Cleveland made a speech expressing the American people's gratitude to the French and promising that the United States would maintain the statue as a worldwide symbol of liberty and friendship for generations to come. Upon the president's conclusion, the crowd clamored for Bartholdi to speak, but he declined. The dedication continued with words from the French consul, W.A. LeFaivre, followed by a speech by the skilled American statesman Chauncey Mitchell Depew on French and American contributions to democracy. The event concluded with a doxology and benediction given by Bishop Henry C. Potter. The grand finale of the day was supposed to be a fireworks display, but due to poor weather conditions this spectacle was postponed until November 1. On that evening, the sky erupted in light to further welcome Liberty to its new home.

Below: Transporting the Statue of Liberty was an honor for the *Isère* and its crew, who spent most of their time moving French troops and supplies from place to place.

Above: The *Isère* entered New York Harbor to great fanfare. An estimated ten thousand people witnessed her arrival.

Below: Crates containing the Statue of Liberty were transferred from the *Isère* to transport boats, which carried the precious cargo to Bedloe's Island for safe storage.

Right: *Scientific American* followed the construction process of the statue, providing its readers with detailed information. These illustrations from the June 13, 1885, issue show the support system used to hold up Liberty and how that framework would be attached to the pedestal.

Opposite: The reassembly process on Bedloe's Island fascinated Americans. General Charles Pomeroy Stone had developed an anchorage structure that consisted of steel beams and tension bars embedded into the pedestal and foundation. The statue's pylon structure—designed by Alexandre-Gustave Eiffel—was then secured to this anchorage. Once Liberty's skeleton was in place, the process of attaching her copper "skin" commenced.

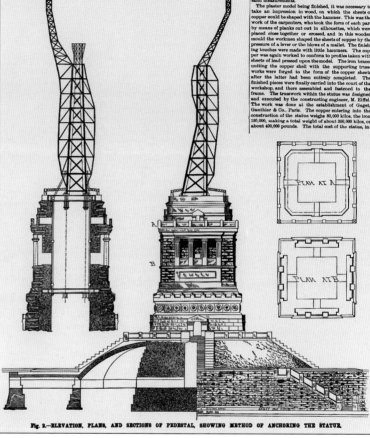

Below: Liberty's feet and her torch's rim await assembly on Bedloe's Island. The man in this photograph gives a good sense of the size of the statue.

Opposite: Liberty's face is ready for installation. Her grand visage is suitable for such a grand lady. Each eye measures two-and-a-half feet (0.76m) across, and her mouth is three feet (0.9m) wide.

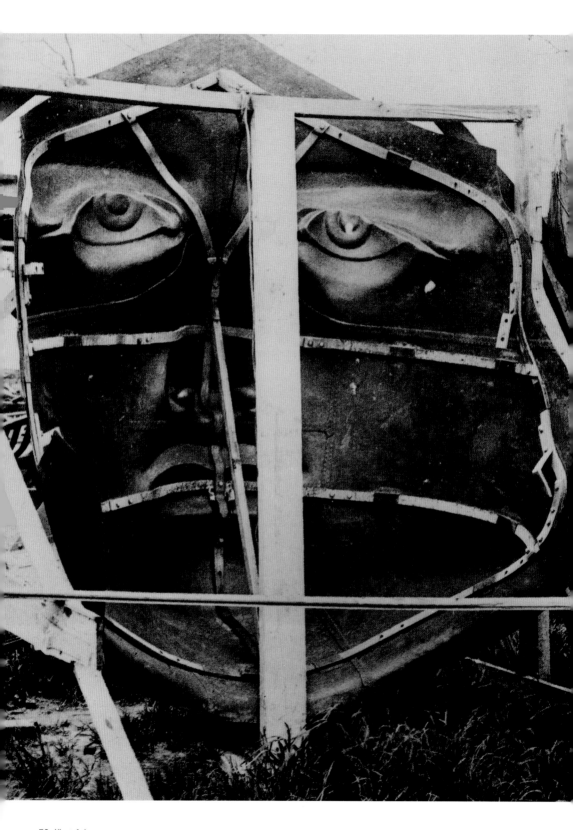

FRANK LESLIE'S ILLUSTRATED NEWSPAPER

No. 1,622.—VOL. LXIII.] NEW YORK—FOR THE WEEK ENDING OCTOBER 23, 1886. [PRICE, 10 CENTS.

Opposite: A look at the reverse side of Liberty's face reveals the iron bars used to support the sheets of copper repoussé. A wooden frame holds the face upright as it awaits attachment to the rest of the statue.

Left: On October 23, 1886—five days before the dedication ceremony—*Frank Leslie's Illustrated Newspaper* published a front cover story on the Statue of Liberty. The American press readily responded to the public's interest in the processes involved in the statue's construction, shipment, and finally, installation.

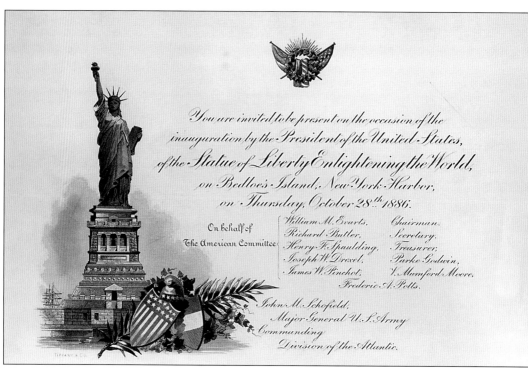

SOUVENIR

PROGRAMME

Of the Unveiling to the Government and Presentation of the United States

Of the Bartholdi

Conceived 1865.

Statue of Liberty

Completed 1886.

ILLUMINATED BY THE AMERICAN SYSTEM OF ELECTRIC LIGHTING.

AT LIBERTY ISLAND,

New York Bay,

OCTOBER 28TH, 1886.

Opposite, top: Bartholdi sketched this image of the way he envisioned Liberty situated in New York Harbor. Note the Brooklyn Bridge under construction in the background to the right.

Opposite, bottom: A limited number of dignitaries received invitations to attend the actual dedication on Bedloe's Island on October 28, 1886. Most spectators watched the festivities aboard small boats or on the shoreline. Joseph Pulitzer hired two steamships for the staff members of the *World* and their families so that they could see the results of their hard work.

Left: The souvenir program included the text of the dedication speeches as well as selected poems and writings about the statue. Notice that the site is referred to as Liberty Island, even though this did not become the official name until 1956. Bartholdi, however, had used this name from the beginning, and the press often followed suit.

Above: Because of poor weather conditions, the grand finale of the dedication ceremonies—a spectacular fireworks show—occurred several days after Liberty's inauguration. Artist Charles Graham created this interpretation of the scene.

Below: An early view, circa 1890, of the completed Statue of Liberty watching over New York Harbor.

Above: The Statue of Liberty was a popular subject for the Detroit Publishing Company, a supplier of postcard views such as this. The docks used by sightseeing ferries are shown in the foreground of the circa 1890s image.

CHAPTER SIX

A Welcoming Sight

In 1883, when the American Committee was in the midst of its pedestal campaign, it organized the Pedestal Art Loan Exhibition, installed at the National Academy of Design in December of that year. Artists and collectors arranged for items to be displayed for two months in order to raise money for the pedestal. There was also to be an auction of art and literary works, and the organizers requested donations from far and wide. Prominent authors such as Mark Twain contributed work, but new writers were also encouraged to participate. One of them, a young poet named Emma Lazarus, wrote a sonnet titled "The New Colossus." She based her work on a comparison between Bartholdi's vision and the legendary Colossus of Rhodes. Dated November 2, 1883, her fourteen-line poem was occasionally published in the years that followed, including during the dedication month of October 1886. Lazarus died the following year, and her work was largely forgotten. In 1888, Houghton Mifflin published a posthumous collection of her poems, including "The New Colossus," but it was not until the twentieth century that this work gained its fame.

Georgina Schuyler, a New York socialite and former friend of Lazarus, happened upon the poem at the beginning of the 1900s. Touched by the words and wanting to honor the memory of her friend, Schuyler recruited the aid of several other people who had known Lazarus. Together they paid for the creation of a bronze tablet inscribed with the words of "The New Colossus." On May 6, 1903, Schuyler and friends presented the tablet to the members of the U.S. Army garrisoned on Bedloe's Island; as the statue's caretakers, they in turn later installed the tablet inside the pedestal for the public to view. It had taken twenty years—as long as it took for the statue to go from concept to reality—but Emma Lazarus's words had become part of the American landscape, particularly the last six lines of the poem:

> "Keep ancient lands, your storied pomp!" cries she
> With silent lips. "Give me your tired, your poor,
> Your huddled masses yearning to breathe free,
> The wretched refuse of your teeming shore,
> Send these, the homeless, tempest-tost to me,
> I lift my lamp beside the golden door."

Right: Emma Lazarus (1849–1887) wrote "The New Colossus" as her contribution to the pedestal campaign. Lazarus was an aid worker on Wards Island and was moved by the plight of the immigrants. That experience, combined with her family's background as descendants of Sephardic Jews who emigrated from Portugal, inspired her to write her sonnet. Lazarus became ill with cancer in 1884 and died a few years later.

When she wrote these words, Lazarus could not have imagined their lasting impact. Even before their placement at the pedestal, her sentiments were being felt by the thousands of immigrants who viewed the statue as they approached the New World. Although subsequent days might prove difficult, as they endured processing through Ellis Island and the trials of adapting to a new land, many would look back with fondness on the welcoming sight of Liberty. The following quotations are taken from immigrants' oral histories compiled by the National Park Service on Ellis Island.

> "And we all got up before daylight....The deck was full of passengers. Everybody went up. The morning was beautiful. And we looked at the Statue of Liberty and honestly we all cried."
>
> 1899—Syrian immigrant

> "I saw the Statue of Liberty. And I said to myself, 'Lady, you're such a beautiful [sic]! You opened your arms, and you get all the foreigners here. Give me a chance to prove that I am worth it, to do something, to become somebody in America.' And always that statue was in my mind."
>
> 1919—Greek immigrant

> "I was choked up with emotion, even though I was only eleven. I saw all those skyscrapers lit up. It was dark. It was wintertime. Little jewels, little twinkles, and the Statue of Liberty within...."
>
> 1939—German immigrant

Above: Many immigrants associated the Statue of Liberty with freedom and unlimited possibilities, echoing the thoughts expressed by Franco-American Union president Ferdinand de Lesseps at the statue's dedication: "In landing beneath its rays, people will know that they have reached a land where individual initiative is developed in all its power." One can only imagine the relief that the immigrants in this circa 1915 photograph felt upon coming to the end of their long journey.

Above: Emma Lazarus's poem "The New Colossus" would come to symbolize the spirit of the Statue of Liberty. Lazarus was encouraged to write something about the statue by her friend Constance Cary Harrison, who was in charge of organizing the Pedestal Art Loan Exhibition of 1883.

Opposite: William Henry Jackson (1843–1942) was a well-known photographer of the American West when he took this shot of the statue in 1892. In 1869, he had photographed construction of the Union Pacific Railroad, and his images of Yellowstone helped prompt Congress's decision to declare it the first National Park in 1872. Jackson was one of the best-known photographers working for the Detroit Publishing Company, the original distributor of this image.

Above: Photographer Edward H. Hart captured this image of the USS *Brooklyn* crossing in front of the statue. Built during 1893–1896, the *Brooklyn* served as the flagship of the Flying Squadron, under the command of Commodore Winfield Scott Schley, in the Spanish-American War. During that conflict, the *Brooklyn* played a key role in the Battle for Santiago on July 3, 1898. Later that year, the ship sailed into New York Harbor for the Spanish-American War Victory Celebration on October 5.

CHAPTER SEVEN

Standing Watch

Day and night, the Statue of Liberty watches over the city, and all of America. As a symbol of freedom, this monument has come to represent patriotism and honor during wartime. Not long after its dedication, the United States became embroiled in the Spanish-American War and the statue shared its waters with battleships. As Liberty stood watch over New York, the military watched over the statue.

Bedloe's Island was a military post from 1811 to 1937. A small fort was built there to defend New York Harbor during the War of 1812, and it was officially named Fort Wood on November 9, 1814, in honor of Lt. Colonel Eleazer D. Wood, hero of the Battle of Lake Erie. For most of the remainder of the nineteenth century, the garrison served as an army recruiting station and ordnance depot. Soldiers stood guard during the construction of the pedestal and the assembly of the statue. From 1904 to 1923, soldiers from the Army Signal Corps were stationed on Bedloe's Island to protect the statue. The corps was eventually replaced by military police, who in turn passed the responsibility on to the National Park Service in 1937. In 1956, on the occasion of the statue's seventieth anniversary, the island changed its name from Bedloe's to Liberty Island.

During wartime, the actual presence and the symbolism of the statue offered comfort to a nation facing hardship. In 1916, President Woodrow Wilson and French ambassador Jean Jules Jusserand participated in the statue's thirtieth anniversary celebration and the installation of a new floodlight system. Europe was on the verge of war, and President Wilson called upon the statue's symbolic importance, stating: "He [President Cleveland] suggested that Liberty enlightening the world would extend her rays from these shores to every other nation. Today that symbolism should be broadened. To the message of liberty which America sends to all the world must be added her message of peace."

"Liberty: The Song of Our Land," composed by Ted S. Barron in 1916, reminded Americans that "Liberty stands for love of our country." It was the first in a series of popular songs written to cheer the home front as the rumblings of war were heard. In April 1917, the United States entered World War I and departing troops most likely knew the tune to the new song "Good-bye Broadway, Hello France," the first lines of which are "Good-bye New York town, good-bye Miss Liberty, Your light of freedom will guide us across the sea." The statue also lent her name and visage to the federal government's "Liberty Loan" campaign for selling war bonds (1917–1918) and the postwar "Victory" promotion of 1919. The public responded, especially to the fund-raising campaigns headed by stars of the silent screen, and more than $23 billion was received for the war effort. At the end of World War I, many returning soldiers' first view of their homeland was the Statue of Liberty as their ships entered New York Harbor.

The Ladies Auxiliary of the Veterans of Foreign Wars took a proprietary interest in the statue. Beginning in 1936, they had participated in the annual rededication ceremonies. During World War II, they were given access to the island, and they used their events to promote patriotism and commitment to the war effort. Liberty's torch was doused not long after the United States entered World War II as part of the national wartime blackouts. Rarely was it relit before the end of the war. The two most notable instances of the torch being lit during this period of darkness marked historic events; the torch shone on June 6, 1944, for fifteen minutes in recognition of the Normandy Invasion, and on May 7, 1945, to recognize the Allies' victory in Europe.

Opposite: The fourth Liberty Loan campaign began on September 28, 1918. It involved a number of fundraising events, including China Day, held in New York City on October 1 of that year. The goal of China Day was to encourage and recognize support from the Chinese-American community. The Chinese government had given its support to the Allied cause earlier in the year by sending laborers to France to assist with the behind-the-lines work so that soldiers could go to the front. In this photograph, participants are dressed to represent China, the Statue of Liberty, and Uncle Sam.

Left: During the 1942 rededication ceremony to celebrate Liberty's fifty-sixth anniversary, the torch was briefly rekindled during the daytime. Seven-year-old Charmaine Stadler (pictured here) did the honors. Her father was in the Fighting French Forces.

Below: The U.S. government mounted a fund-raising campaign during World War I called the "Liberty Loan" program. Bonds were sold in various denominations as a means of financing the war effort. The Statue of Liberty was chosen as the campaign's icon because of its connection with France. This poster, published by Sackett & Wilhelms Corp. of New York, is from the second campaign held in 1917. Alternate versions were printed in Yiddish and Italian.

Above: Photographer Theodor Horydczak shot this view of the Statue of Liberty during the 1920s. Behind the statue are several army buildings that were originally part of Fort Wood. Horydczak is thought to have emigrated from Eastern Europe and to have served with the U.S. Army Signal Corps during World War I. He worked in Washington, D.C., from 1923 to 1959 and is known for his thorough documentation of that city.

Below: On March 27, 1931, Hellmut H. Hellmut (left), a young German radio reporter, conveyed his thoughts about Lady Liberty to listeners in his country via a shortwave hook-up from the statue's crown. The address was also heard across the United States on NBC radio.

Above: Military aircraft, or "war birds," soar over the Statue of Liberty, circa 1935.

Right: The SS *Coamo* is seen leaving New York Harbor in this 1941 image by Jack Delano (1914–1997). The ship, with a capacity of 140 people, was part of the New York and Porto Rico Steamship Line, founded in 1885. First run as a freight operation, the company had branched out into passenger service for immigrants and vacationers by 1900. During World War II, the company's fleet was commissioned into service to provide transport ships. Delano came to the United States from Russia and worked with Roy Stryker of the Farm Security Administration during the Depression. He served as a military photographer during World War II and moved to Puerto Rico upon his discharge.

Right: Andreas Feininger shot this image of the Statue of Liberty against the night-time sky in March 1942. During the first few months following the attack on Pearl Harbor, only a few points of light shone from Liberty's torch and the exterior flood-lights at the site. A full-scale blackout would eventually be imposed as part of national security efforts.

Above: A group of children gaze upon the Statue of Liberty on its fifty-sixth anniversary. The October 1942 ceremony was organized by the American Committee for the Protection of the Foreign Born, an association dedicated to preserving the rights of immigrants. Although popular in 1940 when President Franklin D. Roosevelt addressed the group, the ACPFB came under attack during the McCarthy era, when its members were accused of subversive and un-American activities.

Right, top: Thanks to its success as a national symbol during World War I, the Statue of Liberty was called back into service for World War II. Once again, the statue stood for a patriotic America, strong in the face of foreign aggression. To promote American support for the war effort, the federal government commissioned artwork, such as this 1943 poster by artist Albina Garlinski, in which Liberty shares its space with an aircraft carrier and several biplanes.

Right, bottom: Colonel Fred Boone of Louisville, Kentucky, poses with a group of Bartholdi's models for the Statue of Liberty. Boone was part of a U.S. Army contingent fighting in northeastern France. The photograph was taken on February 17, 1945, at the Bartholdi Museum in Colmar, France—the town in which Bartholdi was born.

LIBERTY FOR ALL

KEEP 'EM FLYING

PENNA ART WPA

Above: A Pan Am flying boat, or Clipper, flies past the Statue of Liberty in this circa 1945 photograph. During World War II, these commercial planes were pressed into military service.

Above: The Statue of Liberty shines in all its glory on May 19, 1945. That evening marked the first time after the attack on Pearl Harbor that the monument was fully illuminated for the entire night.

Above: Crowds gather in Times Square on September 2, 1945, to hear President Truman announce Japan's surrender at the close of World War II. A scaled-down model of the Statue of Liberty presides over the scene.

Above: In 1946, photographer Andreas Feininger captured this serene scene of Liberty standing tall in the midst of a moonlit New York Harbor. All seems still, save for a single tugboat moving along the water.

Left: Photographer Jerry Cooke was on hand in 1946 when these refugee children caught their first sight of the Statue of Liberty.

Below: The Ladies Auxiliary of the Veterans of Foreign Wars has hosted an annual rededication ceremony on the statue's anniversary since 1936. This image was taken in 1947, on the sixty-first anniversary date.

Above: Hungarian immigrants behold the Statue of Liberty as their ship arrives in New York Harbor in 1948.

Above: This image, shot by photographer Herbert Gehr in 1939, reveals the powerful impact that the Statue of Liberty has when fully lit at night.

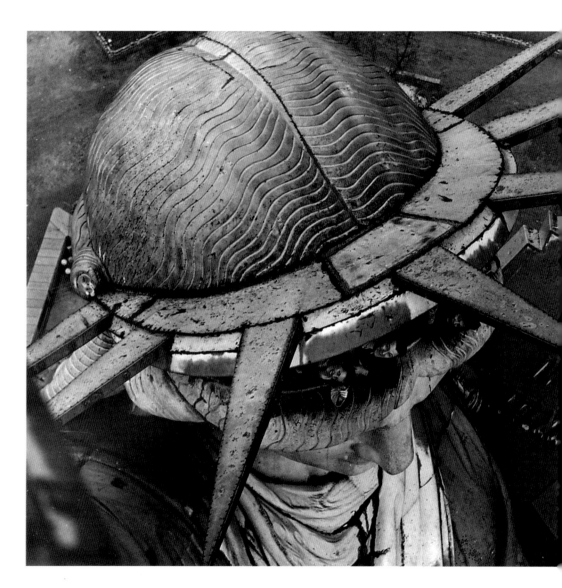

Above: A few brave souls peer out from Liberty's crown toward the camera. After the torch was closed to the public in 1916, the crown became the highest point open to visitors.

CHAPTER EIGHT

Destination Liberty

Even before Liberty's unveiling in 1886, Bedloe's Island was a tourist destination. Boat trips to the site of the Statue of Liberty during the excavation process and the pedestal construction were a popular pastime. Within a year of Liberty's dedication, a visit to the monument was on the "to do" list for New Yorkers and tourists alike. Although its fund-raising duties were over, the American Committee of the Franco-American Union continued its involvement with the statue by supervising the ferry service to and from the island and overseeing the statue's internal maintenance. This continued until 1902, when the army took on the responsibility for access and upkeep—a task ultimately assigned to the National Park Service in 1937.

During the first years after the statue's unveiling, record keeping was sporadic. What numbers exist indicate that about 88,000 people visited Liberty in 1890; following the end of World War I, annual attendance surged above 100,000, with the year 1922 boasting 170,000 visitors. Five hundred thousand people came to the site in 1945, at the end of World War II, and the million mark was surpassed in 1964, which had an attendance record of 1,026,466. Since then, attendance has grown steadily, and now more than 3,000,000 people a year visit Bartholdi's creation.

The views from the Statue of Liberty are spectacular. There is a breathtaking vista from the pedestal's observation balcony located at the statue's feet; on a clear day it is estimated that one can see for fifteen miles (24km) from this point. Visitors also have the option of climbing an additional 162 steps up the spiral staircase to the crown. There, 260 feet (79m) above the sea—at the equivalent height of a twenty-two-story building—visitors have a bird's-eye view of New York Harbor, the five boroughs, and New Jersey. Realizing that the 192 steps from the ground to the pedestal's observation balcony was daunting for some, the army arranged for the Otis Elevator Company to install one of its first cable-operated inventions inside the pedestal during the late autumn of 1906 and into the early part of 1907. That elevator was replaced by an upgraded hydraulic model in 1931. Today, a glass-enclosed double-decker elevator, installed during the 1980s, carries visitors from the ground to the observation balcony, allowing them to see the interior structure and anchorage system of the statue as it is attached to the pedestal.

Over the years, a certain amount of tweaking has been done in the name of improvement, and Liberty's torch has been the subject of many of these efforts. Upon the statue's opening, visitors had access to the torch via a service entrance located at the statue's shoulder.

Entering through a small door, they could climb a narrow forty-two-
foot (12.8m) ladder to the torch's observation deck, which rested
three hundred feet (91.4m) above the ground. Basically a catwalk, this
deck could accommodate approximately twelve people at a time. The
torch was closed off to the public on July 30, 1916, as a result of the
Black Tom explosion—an incident during which barges and railroad
cars loaded with munitions and dynamite exploded at the Lehigh
Valley Railroad terminal located on Black Tom Island, New Jersey,
next to Bedloe's Island. Although damage to the statue was limited to
surface nicks and the popping of rivets, primarily on the right arm,
the entire statue—along with the rest of Bedloe's Island—was closed
for inspection for ten days before reopening on August 10.

Early on, Liberty's keepers had decided to "improve" upon
Bartholdi's original idea of a torch boasting a gilt-finished flame lit
from underneath. Instead of merely shining a light upon the flame,
the American Committee had it electrified from within. During
autumn of 1886, portholes were cut into the copper flame and nine
arc lamps were installed inside. However, the visual result was considered unsatisfying, so further modification occurred in 1892 with
the enlargement of the portholes and the addition of a glass skylight.
This degree of illumination was not enough to please critics either,
so in 1916, following the Black Tom explosion, American artist
Gutzon Borglum, creator of Mount Rushmore, gave the torch a major
design overhaul, resulting in what some have referred to as a
"Chinese lantern effect." He accomplished this by removing much of
the copper from the flame and replacing it with amber-colored glass.
Borglum's modifications had the unfortunate consequence of creating
a series of leaks, leading to internal corrosion and ultimately the
total replacement of the torch in the 1980s. That later renovation
restored the original concept of a gilded flame bearing a solid surface
and lit by spotlights.

On October 15, 1924, the Statue of Liberty was declared a national monument by the United States government, and in 1933, responsibility for her care and upkeep was transferred to the Department of
the Interior. One of the department's first acts was to begin cleaning
the statue for its golden anniversary in 1936. Liberty was indeed
beginning to show wear and tear. In 1937–39, a major restoration in
preparation for the 1939 World's Fair in New York took place under
the auspices of the Public Works Administration (PWA) and the
Works Progress Administration (WPA). Repairs were made to the
crown's support system, rusted cast-iron steps were replaced by rein-
forced concrete, and sections of corroded armature were removed.
This work required the closing of the statue to the public from May
through December of 1938. During this first restoration, much of the
old army facility was demolished, and improvements were made to
the docks and entrance facilities. Liberty underwent another major
overhaul in preparation for its one-hundredth birthday. In May 1982,
President Ronald Reagan authorized the creation of the Statue of

Liberty–Ellis Island Centennial Committee and gave it the task of coordinating activities leading up to the anniversary celebrations at both sites—1986 for the statue and 1992 for Ellis Island. The statue was closed to the public from August 1985 through June 1986. During this time, its internal armature structure was replaced, as were the thousands of rivets holding the copper repoussé sheets in position. Liberty underwent cosmetic "surgery" on her face, with repairs to one nostril, her right eye, and her lips and chin. The torch was completely replaced, and the statue received an overall pressure cleaning. By the end of June, it was ready for unveiling.

July 3 through 6, 1986, was designated "Liberty Weekend" in New York in honor of the statue's centennial. Operation Sail, with its parade of tall ships from around the world, made a return appearance in New York Harbor—its first visit since the bicentennial celebrations of 1976. President Reagan served as the nation's master of ceremonies for the event and was on hand, along with French president François Mitterand, for the rededication service. During the statue's unveiling on July 4, 1986, President Reagan proclaimed: "We are the keepers of the flame of liberty; we hold it high for the world to see."

Since the beginning, the Statue of Liberty has represented those desiring a better world. On October 28, 1886—during the statue's dedication ceremony—suffragists protested from a chartered boat in the waters off Bedloe's Island. They were troubled that only two women—Bartholdi's wife and Lesseps's teenage daughter—were included among the more than two thousand invited guests in attendance on the island for the festivities. Even more disturbing was the fact that a woman was being used for the nation's symbol of liberty, yet in the United States, women, who at the time were denied the right to vote, didn't have political independence. During the twentieth century, the statue and her island bore witness to various civil rights and antiwar demonstrations. In 1989, she served as inspiration to the Chinese students protesting for democracy in Tiananmen Square who modeled their "Goddess of Democracy" after her. As Bartholdi foresaw, she has achieved immortality in an otherwise transitory world. Today, Liberty still watches over New York Harbor. Her presence, even in the darkest days, continues to offer comfort and hope.

Right: The Hudson-Fulton Celebration of 1909 commemorated the three-hundredth anniversary of Henry Hudson's exploration of the New York river that came to bear his name and the one-hundredth anniversary of Robert Fulton's first successful use of steam-powered watercraft. The Statue of Liberty was spruced up for the occasion with additional illumination.

Opposite, top: In 1909, aviation pioneer Wilbur Wright took off from Governor's Island, crossed the harbor, and circled the Statue of Liberty before flying up the Hudson River to Grant's Tomb and back as part of the Hudson-Fulton Celebration.

Opposite, bottom: From the beginning, the Statue of Liberty was closely tied with tourism. The advertisement on the left side of this pamphlet tempts visitors with ease of access to the island, the lure of "fresh air," dining opportunities, and the promise of security. On the right side is statistical information about the statue, which provided interesting reading during the ferry ride.

 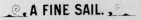

Above: This circa 1925 image shows a view of Manhattan from the Statue of Liberty's pedestal. From the higher vantage point of the crown, visitors are granted an unparalleled vista of all five boroughs and New Jersey; on a clear day, one can see as far as twenty or so miles (32.2km).

Opposite: Visitors head toward the statue after disembarking from the ferry in this June 20, 1946, photograph. The increased number of people who came to the site after World War II caused guards to complain about litter and other unpleasant marks left behind by the tourists.

Opposite: Visitors climb the double spiral staircase—consisting of 162 steps—located inside the statue itself. In total, there are 354 steps that go from the ground entrance, through the pedestal, and up the statue to the crown.

Above: The statue's caretakers have struggled for years with visitors who feel compelled to leave their mark or message somewhere inside the statue. Periodic cleanups help, but graffiti—like that shown in this June 20, 1946, image—has always been a problem.

Above: Schoolboy Paul Mayo does his homework during his commute to school from Bedloe's Island in the 1950s. Beginning in the 1930s, various National Park Service employees and their families lived in the shadow of the Statue of Liberty. In 1952, they were provided with new brick residences on the western portion of Bedloe's Island, but schooling still took place on Governor's Island.

Below: A group of schoolchildren stand in front of the Statue of Liberty during the 1950s. Class field trips to the statue are common excursions.

Below: Circle Line ferries have provided transportation to and from the statue since 1945. Today, they offer visitors access from New Jersey as well as Lower Manhattan.

Above: In this 1956 image, the *Île de France* ocean liner sails past the Statue of Liberty. Governor's Island and Brooklyn can be seen in the background.

Below: Who is this woman standing tall with the Statue of Liberty? On October 10, 1956, the *New York Times* reported that National Park Service officials were searching for a female descendant of Bartholdi in anticipation of the statue's seventieth anniversary celebration. The 1956 event would also recognize the renaming of Bedloe's Island to Liberty Island—a name that had first been proposed by Bartholdi himself. In this photograph's original caption information, dated November 1956, the woman is identified as Bartholdi's "great granddaughter"—yet he and Jeanne-Emilie never had children. Despite extensive research, her identity remains a mystery.

Above: Photographer Henry Grossman took this 1960 photograph of a soon-to-be president—John F. Kennedy—and the Statue of Liberty.

Opposite: Not only has the Statue of Liberty been a tourist attraction, but it has also been the backdrop for numerous political and social demonstrations. Here, singer Harry Belafonte gives a speech at a civil rights rally held at the Statue of Liberty in May 1960. Photographer Al Fenn documented the event.

Right: The women's rights movement has had a long-standing connection with the monument, beginning with the statue's dedication day in 1886 when suffragists protested that only two women were included among the two thousand invited guests at the ceremony on Bedloe's Island. In 1915, suffragists staged a demonstration in favor of women's voting rights. The women pictured here on August 10, 1970, are rallying in support of the Equal Rights Amendment.

Left: A fife and drum corps stands at attention during the seventy-sixth anniversary of the statue on October 28, 1962.

Below: During America's bicentennial in 1976, Operation Sail filled New York Harbor with tall ships from around the world. This parade of vessels was led by the U.S. Coast Guard *Eagle*. In the midst of this celebration of independence, the Statue of Liberty stood tall as a fitting symbol.

Opposite: Photographer Fred R. Conrad framed the Statue of Liberty between the twin towers of the World Trade Center in 1983. The photograph now resonates as a fitting reminder of the power of liberty in the face of adversity.

Above: An aerial view of the Statue of Liberty reveals the star-shaped courtyard in which the monument is situated.

Sources

BOOKS

Numerous books have been written about the Statue of Liberty. The following publications were used in the research for this book and may prove interesting for further reading:

Aguila, Dani, comp. and ed. *Taking Liberty with the Lady, by Cartoonists from Around the World*. Nashville: Eagle Nest Press, 1986.

Bartholdi, Frédéric-Auguste. *The Statue of Liberty Enlightening the World*. New York: North American Review, 1885.

Brian, Denis. *Pulitzer: A Life*. New York: John Wiley & Sons, Inc., 2001.

Burchard, Sue. *The Statue of Liberty: Birth to Rebirth*. New York: Harcourt Brace Jovanovich, Publishers, 1985.

Causel, Laurent. *Bartholdi and the Statue of Liberty—Centennial Commemoration*. Strasbourg, France: Editions de la Nuée-Bleue, 1984.

Dillon, Wilton S., and Neil G. Kotler, eds. *The Statue of Liberty Revisited: Making a Universal Symbol*. Washington, D.C.: Smithsonian Institution Press, 1994.

Fox, Nancy Jo. *Liberties with Liberty: The Fascinating Story of America's Proudest Symbol*. New York: Dutton, 1986.

Gibson, Henry. *The Gift: The Illustrated History of the Statue of Liberty*. El Cajon, Calif.: Blackthorne, 1986.

Jackson, Kenneth T., ed. *The Encyclopedia of New York City*. New Haven, Conn.: Yale University Press, 1995.

Mercer, Charles. *Statue of Liberty*. New York: G.P. Putnam's Sons, 1979.

Moreno, Barry. *The Statue of Liberty Encyclopedia*. New York: Simon & Schuster, 2000.

New York Public Library. *Liberty: The French-American Statue in Art and History*. New York: Harper & Row Publishers, 1986.

O'Brien, Maureen C. *In Support of Liberty: European Paintings at the 1883 Pedestal Art Loan Exhibition*. New York: Parrish Art Museum and National Academy of Design, 1986.

Trachtenberg, Marvin. *The Statue of Liberty*. New York: Viking Press, 1976.

WEBSITES

www.ellisisland.org   Statue of Liberty-Ellis Island Foundation, Inc.

www.mcny.org   The Museum of the City of New York

www.nyhistory.org   The New-York Historical Society

www.nypl.org   The New York Public Library

www.nps.gov/elis   Ellis Island National Monument

www.nps.gov/stli   Statue of Liberty National Monument

Photo Credits

Bartholdi Museum: ©Christian KEMPF: p. 11; 19, 21, 23

Brown Brothers: p. 24-25, 108, 109 top, 116

Corbis : p. 5-6, 30, 38, 39, 72 bottom, 112, 122 bottom; ©Bettmann: p. 12, 73, 78, 80, 88, 93, 99, 105, 110, 111, 113, 122 top; ©Dave G. Houser: 2-3, 107; ©Gail Mooney: p. 124; ©Parsons & Atwater: p. 20 bottom; ©Richard Morris Hunt: p.121

Hulton Achive/Getty Images: p. 13, 85, 89, 96, 97, 100, 102-103, 114, 115, 117; ©Dave G. Houser: p. 107; ©Edwin Levick: 79, 95; ©Hulton-Deutsch Collection: p. 105

Library of Congress: p. 86-87; ©Jack Delano: p. 90-91; p. 87 ©Detroit Publishing Company: p. 76-77; ©Albina Garlinski, lithographer: p. 94 top; ©Edward H. Hart: p. 82-83; ©William Henry Jackson: p. 81; ©Henry Greenwood Peabody: p. 8-9

Museum of the City of New York: p. 62; Gift of Estelle Cameron Silo in memory of her Husband James Patrick Silo: p. 22

National Park Service: p. 4-5, 10 left and right, 15, 16-17, 18, 20 top, 26, 27, 28, 31, 32, 32-33, 34, 35, 36-37, 40-41, 42, 43, 44, 45, 47, 48-49, 50, 52-53, 54, 55 top, 60-61, 63, 64, 65, 66, 68, 69, 70, 71, 72 top, 75, 86, 94 bottom, 109 bottom;

©Associated Press: p. 67; ©Charles Graham: p. 74; ©National Archives: p. 46

New York Public Library: p. 55 bottom

The New York Times: ©Fred R. Conrad: p. 123

Timepix: ©George B. Brainerd: p. 56, 57; ©Jerry Cooke: p. 99 top; ©Bill Eppridge: p. 14; ©Andreas Feininger: p. 92, 98; ©Al Fenn: p. 120; ©Herbert Gehr: p. 118; ©Henry Grossman: p. 119; ©Wallace G. Levinson: p. 58-59; ©Sharland: p. 101; ©Underwood & Underwood/War Department/National Archives: p. 84

Index

American Committee for the
Protection of the Foreign Born,
93
American Committee of the Franco-
American Union, 29, 43,
49–51, *54*, 103
American Revolution, 9
Amérique, 61
anniversary ceremonies, 84, *85, 93,
99*, 104–106, *107*, 118, *122*
Atwater, Lyman, 21

Barron, Ted S., 83
Bartholdi, Charlotte, *18*, 19
Bartholdi, Frédéric-Auguste, 9–10,
10, 16, 17, 19, 26–26, 29,
37–38, *39*, 61–62
Bartholdi Museum, 94
Battle of Lake Erie, 83
Bedloe's Island, *20*, 26, 49, 58–59,
62, 114. *See also* Fort Wood;
Liberty Island
Belafonte, Harry, *120*
bicentennial celebration, 106, *122*
Black Tom explosion, 104
Boone, Fred, *94*
Borglum, Gutzon, 104
Boston, 49
Brainerd, George B., 56, 57
Brodie, William A., 50
Brooklyn Bridge, 72

Casino Theatre, 54
centennial celebration, 104–106,
107
Champs de Mars, 29
China Day, *84*
Chrysler Building, 37
civil rights rally, *120*, 121
Civil War, 9
Cleveland, Grover, 62, 63
Colossus of Rhodes, 25, 77
*Comité français pour l'émancipa-
tion des esclaves*, 9
Conrad, Fred R., 122
Cooke, Jerry, 99
crown, 29, *102*, 103, 104
early model of, *22*

Declaration of Independence, 12
Delano, Jack, 90
Depew, Chauncey Mitchell, 63
Detroit Publishing Company, 76, 80
du Puysieux, Jeanne-Emilie Baheux,
29

*L'Égypte apportant la lumière à
l'Asie*, 9, *11*

Eiffel, Alexandre-Gustave, 30, 37,
38, 66
Eiffel Tower, 37, 39
elevator, 103
Ellis Island, 78, 106
Equal Rights Amendment, 121
Evarts, Williams M., 43

face, *69, 70*
feet, *45, 68*
Feininger, Andreas, 92, 98
Fenn, Al, 121
ferry service, *56, 76*, 103
floodlight system, 83, *92*
Fort Wood, 49, 83, 87
framework, 37–39, *66*
Franco-American Union, 25, 26–29,
32, 39, 47
Franco-Prussian War, 10
*Frank Leslie's Illustrated
Newspaper, 47, 71*
"Freedom of the City," 61
Freemasons, 50
French Committee of the Franco-
American Union, 29
fund-raising campaigns, 25–30, 34,
49–51, 54, *55, 56*

Gaget, Emile, 30
Gaget, Gauthier et Companie, 30,
39, *47*
Garlinski, Albina, 94
Gasparin, Agénor de, 9
Gauthier, J.B., 30
Gehr, Herbert, 100
Goddess of Democracy, 106
"Good-bye Broadway, Hello
France," 83
Governor's Island, *108*, 114
Grace, William R., 61
graffiti, *113*
Graham, Charles, *74*
Grant, Ulysses S., 17, *29, 33*
Grant's Tomb, 108
Grossman, Henry, 119

Harrison, Benjamin, 47
Harrison, Constance Cary, 80
Hart, Edward H., 82
head
attachment of, 61
construction of, 29, *34*
design of, 19, 29
display of, *42*
model of, 40–41
at Paris Universal Exhibition, 29,
34, *35*
Hellmut, Hellmut H., 88

Histoire des États-Unis, 9
Horydczak, Theodor, 87
Hôtel du Louvre, 25
Hudson-Fulton Celebration, *108,
109*
Hugo, Victor, 44
Hunt, Richard Morris, 49–50

Île des Cygnes, 13
immigrants, 78, *79, 99, 100*
Isère, 61, *62, 63, 64*, 65

Jackson, William Henry, 80
Journal Universel, 34
Jusserand, Jean Jules, 83

Kennedy, John F., *119*

La Farge, John, 17
Laboulaye, Édouard-René Lefebvre
de, 9–10, *10*, 17, 19, 25, 39
Ladies Auxiliary of the Veterans of
Foreign Wars, 83–84, 99
Lafayette, Marquis de, 26
Lazarus, Emma, 77–78, *78*, 80
LeFaivre, W.A., 63
Lesseps, Ferdinand Marie de, 39, 63,
79
Levison, Wallace G., *57, 59*
Libertas, 17–18
*Liberté éclairant le monde. See
Statue of Liberty*
Liberty Island, *73, 83*, 118. *See also*
Bedloe's Island
Liberty Loan campaign, 83, *84, 86*
"Liberty: The Song of Our Land," 83
Liberty Weekend, 106, *107*
Lincoln, Abraham, 9
Longfellow, Henry Wadsworth, 17

Madison Square Park, *24*, 29, *31*, 62
Martin, Henri, 9
Mayo, Paul, *114*
military, *14*, 83, *89, 94, 95. See also*
Fort Wood
Mitterand, François, 106
Modèle du Comité, 32
Monduit and Béchet, 19, 29, *33*
Morton, Levi Parsons, 39, 43, 47
Mount Rushmore, 104

National Academy of Design, 77
National Park Service, 83, 103, 114
"The New Colossus," 77–78, *80*
New York Harbor, *8*, 17, *20*, 58–59,
83
New York Times, 49, 62
New York Tribune, 25

New York World, 50–51, *55*, 73
nimbus, *105*
Normandy Invasion, 84
Nôtre Dame Cathedral, 26

observation balcony, 103, *110*
Olmsted, Frederick Law, 61
Operation Sail, 106, *122*
Otis Elevator Company, 103

Paris Universal Exhibition, 29, 34, 35
Parsons, Charles R., 20
Pasha, Isma'il, 9
Peabody, George Greenwood, 8
pedestal
    construction of, *48*, 49–51, *50*, *53*
    fund-raising for, 26, 49, 77, 80
    observation balcony of, 103, *110*
Pedestal Art Loan Exhibition, 77, 80
Philadelphia Centennial Exhibition, 26, *27*, *30*
pointing, 37
political demonstrations, *120*
Pont de Grenelle, *13*
Port of New York: Bird's Eye View from the Battery Looking South, 20
Potter, Henry C., 63
Public Works Administration, 104
Pulitzer, Joseph, 50–51, *55*, 73

Reagan, Ronald, 104–106
rededication. *See* anniversary ceremonies
Rémusat, Charles de, 9
repoussé, 26, *36*, 37

Sackett & Wilhelms Corp., 84
Schley, Winfield Scott, 82
Schuyler, Georgina, 77
Scientific American, 66
Second Continental Congress, 12

Secrétan, Pierre-Eugène, 36
shackles, 19
Simon, Marie, 37
slavery, 9, 19
social demonstrations, *120*
Spanish-American War, 82, 83
SS *Coamo*, 90, *90–91*
Stadler, Charmaine, *85*
staircase, 103, 104, *112*
Staten Island, *20*
Statue of Liberty. *See also* pedestal; torch
    acceptance of, 29, *64*, 65
    arrival of, 61, *62*
    assembly of, 37–39, *43*, *44*
    completion of, 39
    copy of, *13*
    crown of, *22*, *102*
    dedication of, *60*, 62–63, *72*, 73, *74*
    design of, 17–19, *19*
    elevator in, 103
    face of, *69*, 70
    feet of, *45*, 68
    framework for, 37–39, 66
    graffiti in, *113*
    head of, 19, 29, *34*, *35*, *42*, 61
    illumination of, *15*, 83, *92*, *101*
    inspiration for, 9–10
    installation of, 61, *67*
    models of, 19, *21–23*, *32*, 37, *39–41*, *94*
    nimbus of, *105*
    presentation of, *46*, 47
    restoration of, 104–106, *105*
    shackles and, 19
    staircase in, 103, 104, *112*
    tablet of law of, *12*, *23*
    World War II and, 90, *92*, *94*, *96*, *97*
Stone, Charles Pomeroy, 61–62, 66
Storrs, Richard S., 63
Stryker, Roy, 90

Suez Canal, 9, 11
Sumner, Charles, 17

tablet of law, *12*, *23*
Thiébaut Frères, 13
Tiananmen Square, 106
Tocqueville, Alexis de, 17
torch
    assembly of, *68*
    design of, *21*
    in Madison Square Park, *24*, *31*
    in Philadelphia, 24, *27*, *30*
    renovation of, 103–104
    World War II and, 84, *85*, *92*, *96*
tourism, 103, *109*, *110*, *111*, *112*, *115*
Twain, Mark, 77

Union League, 29
Union Pacific Railroad, 80
USS *Brooklyn*, 82

Viollet-le-Duc, Eugène-Emmanuel, 26, 30

War of 1812, 83
war bonds, 83, 84, 86
Wards Island, 78
Wilson, Woodrow, 83
women's rights movement, 106, *121*
Wood, Eleazer D., 83
Works Progress Administration, 104
World Trade Center, *123*
World War I, 83–84
World War II, 84, *85*, 90, *92*, 94
World's Fair, 37, 39, 104
Wright, Wilbur, 108

Yellowstone National Park, 80
Young, Brigham, 17